NUAL 2013

MATCH OF THE **DAY**

THIS ANNUAL BELONGS TO:

AGE:

MY FAVOURITE TEAM IS:

MY FAVOURITE PLAYER IS:

MY FOOTY DREAM IS:

MUM & DAD KEEP OUT!

Turn over to see what's **INSIDE!**

WELCOME

Your Match of the Day Annual 2013 is packed full of fun, quizzes, facts, superstars and pictures from another amazing year of footy. Enjoy it, readers!

GARY LINEKER

INSIDE YOUR ANNUAL!

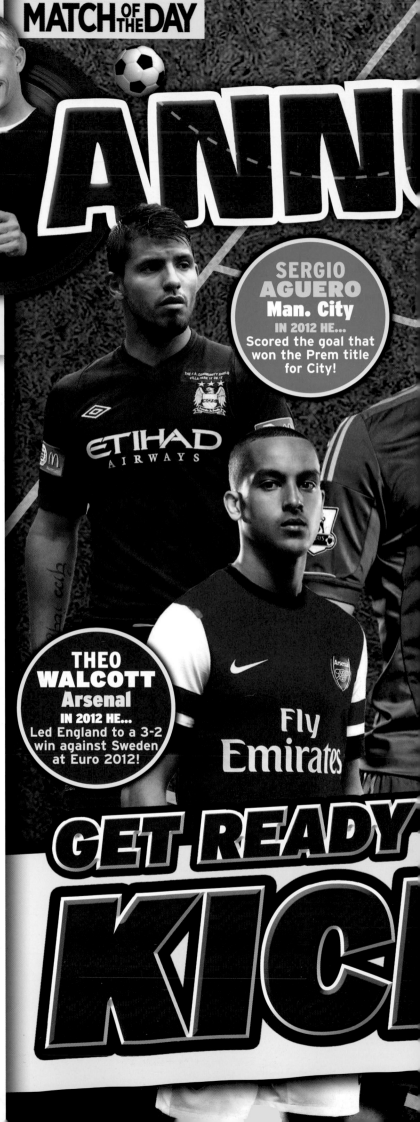

MATCH OF THE DAY

ANNU

SERGIO AGUERO
Man. City
IN 2012 HE...
Scored the goal that won the Prem title for City!

THEO WALCOTT
Arsenal
IN 2012 HE...
Led England to a 3-2 win against Sweden at Euro 2012!

GET READY

KICI

UAL 2013

FOR... K-OFF!

All these stars and more are in your awesome Annual

GARETH BALE
Tottenham
IN 2012 HE...
Signed a big new four-year contract at Spurs!

WAYNE ROONEY
Man. United
IN 2012 HE...
Celebrated ten years as England's hottest striker!

LIONEL MESSI
Barcelona
IN 2012 HE...
Bagged an amazing 50 league goals for Barcelona!

FERNANDO TORRES
Chelsea
IN 2012 HE...
Helped The Blues to win the Champions League final!

SUPER

What out for these young stars in 2013!

5

4

3

LUCAS PIAZON
Chelsea   Age: 18

SKILL	86
SPEED	86
STRENGTH	85
SHOOTING	87
PASSING	88
AVERAGE	86

The teenage star wants to feature in The Blues' senior side this season after impressing with the youth team. He's got bags of talent – if he gets a chance, he'll take it!

RAHEEM STERLING
Liverpool   Age: 17

SKILL	89
SPEED	90
STRENGTH	84
SHOOTING	84
PASSING	85
AVERAGE	86

Liverpool fans have been shouting about this goalscoring winger for ages. We reckon 2013 will be his breakthrough year – rival defenders won't live with his speed and skills!

ROSS BARKLEY
Everton   Age: 18

SKILL	85
SPEED	85
STRENGTH	93
SHOOTING	89
PASSING	90
AVERAGE	88

Everton have big hopes for powerful England Under-21 midfielder Ross Barkley. Just like ex-team-mate Jack Rodwell, he's cool, clever, energetic and destined for the top!

EST·1892

KIDS

2

NICK POWELL
Man. United Age: 18

POWELL 25

SKILL	90
SPEED	89
STRENGTH	90
SHOOTING	93
PASSING	90
AVERAGE	**90**

After teenage forward Powell scored a spectacular goal for Crewe at Wembley last summer, United moved quickly to snap him up. He'll be awesome taking on defences with Rooney and Welbeck in the future!

1

Fly Emirates

SUPERKID! No.1 SUPERKID!

ALEX OXLADE-CHAMBERLAIN
Arsenal Age: 19

SKILL	88
SPEED	89
STRENGTH	92
SHOOTING	91
PASSING	89
AVERAGE	**90**

2013 is gonna be the year of The Ox! The Arsenal and England midfielder has stacks of skill, confidence and technique to rip it up in the Prem and rock the Champions League!

MEGA WOR

Can you find these 20 goal kings hiding in this grid? You'll get

```
O O E K A K O P Q Z M K N K C F M H T P B U H J N
B G Y D W T Y E Y L A P A F B I E I A Y I Z D X I
D Z W W M E S S I Y X D V A P F X X E I J G I H Z
B M P L L V Y L X F M O F S J S Y D J W H H M M
D Q D T G E O G A H Q Q A L I I L Y P B O S E Y B
E U G K R Z D H C A Z A F P V V A G U E R O W B U
D E R B L W L P I A E I T F X W R Z D T S C F A D
X N U A X G A Z J M R A Z T D V V W N X N F R E
L Q Z L X B N M J X A R T I P E S U W E K W A W H
S Q R U Z X O N N V U D O A O F R K C B N J L D R
R U Y D V L R E Y C S S N L P S O A F S J Z L A G
B K H K U P E G M B N N H R L U B X H D A I I M Y
J A J N E I S R E P N A V N I D K E S F N Q V B E
E R L D H G V B W P K M W Q Y P R O N H U R K L N
Q Q E O D F X A W L U A U V L N D O Z Z A C I I O
L L Q X T Y G J Q E J J T R A R V K G Z E Y T J O
G O A O O E A H E W K B D N X T O T D B P M S G R
O R M J J O L I W J S U D N V S O Y R S A P A A Q
M Q O R N E G L M N Z E M L M X L R A L D Z A O F
E E O E T L P V I V Z P O T F B F U R B S L X F E
Z Q M H H V R E P F T B X C D A S K E E E R W W T
A R W E G K G V D E U R M G Z Q O T S D A X K
O S C I S S E B V R Q A N B M J B V N J X M A T N
N A L R O F U B E X F B T B L V S U M H R P A K Y
N K K J N C X W D Q Z I P G B P H G O Y I W R N U
```

MY SCORE OUT OF 100

RDSEARCH!

five points for each one!

Rooney
Van Persie
Messi
Tevez
Ronaldo
Gomez
Hernandez
Benzema
Cisse
Adebayor
Torres
Carroll
Drogba
Balotelli
Aguero
Huntelaar
Suarez
Forlan
Villa
Bent

Aguero

Gomez

Benzema

Hernandez

Van Persie

ANSWERS

More Quiz Fun on p16!

11

 2012 SUPERSTAR!

 STAR FACTS

POSITION: Striker
VALUE: £40m
DID YOU KNOW? In 2012, Wazza played his 500th senior game aged just 26!

ROONEY

 MAN. UNITED & ENGLAND

Paz &

PAZ!

BEZ!

Check out some of the big stars the MOTD Kickabout reporters hung out with this year!

Hey Leo, fancy a rematch?

Si Paz, and this time I win 7-0!

LIONEL MESSI
PAZ SAYS: "Meeting Messi was awesome. We had a great laugh and even played FIFA – I beat him 1-0, which was a bit of a shock!"

WAYNE ROONEY
PAZ SAYS: "The Man. United legend was a top bloke. We chatted about what he was like at school, getting told off by his mum and the nicknames his mates call him!"

How does my hair look, Ash?

Man up, Bez!

ASHLEY YOUNG
BEZ SAYS: "I did some training exercises with Ash before Euro 2012. Man, that was really hard work – his fitness was sooo good!"

Bez

"Our best footy friends in 2012!"

Hey Bez, are we a bit overdressed?

Nah, Paz. Suits you!

JERMAIN DEFOE

BEZ SAYS: "We met up with JD at a charity footy event. He told me that Robin van Persie, who was his Arsenal rival back then, was the hottest striker in the Prem!"

I thought you were Ant & Dec!

DJIBRIL CISSE

PAZ SAYS: "We sat down for a cup of tea and a slice of cake with the crazy QPR striker in London. The flashy Frenchman revealed he's designing his own clothes range!"

ASHLEY COLE

BEZ SAYS: "Cole told me he really enjoys playing for England. A couple of weeks later, his penalty miss against Italy helped knock England out of Euro 2012. Doh!"

I say, Djib old chap, what a nice cuppa!

Bad joke, Paz!

It's the only cup QPR will get this year!

Catch Paz & Bez on **MOTD KICKABOUT** Saturday mornings on CBBC and BBC Two!

15

GUESS WHO!

Name these mystery stars and get five points for each one!

1 ANSWER

2 ANSWER

3 ANSWER

4 ANSWER

5 ANSWER

6 ANSWER

7 ANSWER

8 ANSWER

9 ANSWER

10 ANSWER

11 ANSWER

12 ANSWER

ANSWERS: 1. Darren Bent, 2. Sergio Aguero, 3. Nikica Jelavic, 4. Danny Welbeck, 5. Lionel Messi, 6. Frank Lampard, 7. Steven Gerrard, 8. Fernando Torres, 9. Cristiano Ronaldo, 10. Wayne Rooney, 11. Cesc Fabregas, 12. Mario Balotelli.

MY SCORE OUT OF 60

More Quiz Fun on p26!

16

2012 SUPERSTAR!

STAR FACTS

POSITION: Forward
VALUE: £100 million
DID YOU KNOW? In 2012, Ron became the only player to twice score 40 Spanish league goals!

RONALDO

REAL MADRID & PORTUGAL

PREMIER LEAGUE TEAM OF THE YEAR!

Goalkeeper
Joe Hart
Man. City
Hart is clearly the No.1 choice for the keeper's spot in the MOTD Team of the Year. City let in the fewest goals last season – mainly thanks to this guy!
Top skill: Making flying wonder-saves!

Right-back
Micah Richards
Man. City
Micah missed out on Euro 2012 – but he was good enough to win the Prem title with City!
Top skill: Using his mega strength!

Centre-back
Vincent Kompany
Man. City
City aren't the same team when captain Vinnie isn't in their defence. He's strong, quick, clever, calm, skilful – he's worth his weight in gold!
Top skill: Powering over strikers to head the ball clear!

Centre-back
Jonny Evans
Man. United
Surprised? You shouldn't be! Jonny has been awesome in 2012 and United boss Alex Ferguson thinks he's now one of the best defenders in the Prem!
Top skill: Stealing the ball from attackers!

Left-back
Ashley Cole
Chelsea
Ash is one of the best left-backs ever, and in 2012 he picked up his seventh FA Cup medal and won the Champions League for the first time. He could play in any team in the world!
Top skill: Sticking to opposition attackers like glue!

Midfielder
Yaya Toure
Man. City

Yaya scores, tackles, runs and passes like some kind of midfield machine. Without him, City wouldn't have won the title!
Top skill: Match-winning goals!

Midfielder
David Silva
Man. City

The silky Spaniard can run a game all by himself – his vision, speed, technique and shooting is deadly. Set up 17 Prem goals last season!
Top skill: Super-slick footwork!

Midfielder
Gareth Bale
Tottenham

He's got the best left foot in the Prem and Spurs are such an attacking force when Bale rips down the wing!
Top skill: Zooming past defenders like a robot!

Striker
Wayne Rooney
Man. United

Though he didn't win a trophy in 2012, it was probably his best year on the pitch with 27 Prem goals and a string of world-class games!
Top skill: Wicked long-range shooting!

Striker
Robin van Persie
Man. United

With 30 Prem goals in the 2011-12 season, it's no surprise why Man. United paid Arsenal more than £20 million for RVP!
Top skill: Left-foot screamers!

Striker
Sergio Aguero
Man. City

What a debut season for Aguero at City. He's a club legend after scoring the goal that won the title and the £34 million that City paid looks a proper bargain!
Top skill: Scoring goals in tight situations!

Turn over to see the team in action!

PREMIER LEAGUE

TEAM OF THE YEAR!

Check out our superstar Prem team!

Micah Richards
Club Man. City
RATING 8/10

David Silva
Club Man. City
RATING 9/10

Wayne Rooney
Club Man. United
RATING 9/10

Drops deep to set up attacks
– and scores wonder goals!

Sergio Aguero
Club Man. City
RATING 9/10

MANAGER OF THE YEAR!
David Moyes Everton
He hasn't had much to spend on players,
but Moyesey kept The Toffees in contention
for a European spot against all the odds!

Jonny Evans
Club Man. United
RATING 8/10

Joe Hart
Club Man. City
RATING 9/10

Vincent Kompany
Club Man. City
RATING 9/10

Ashley Cole
Club Chelsea
RATING 9/10

Big, powerful and wins loads of headers!

Amazing finger-tip saves and accurate distribution!

Looks to attack at every opportunity!

Yaya Toure
Club Man. City
RATING 9/10

...gh holding midfielder ...o also launches attacks!

Bombs into the box and whips in deadly crosses!

Gareth Bale
Club Tottenham
RATING 8/10

SUBSTITUTES

Petr Cech
Club Chelsea
Keeper

Kyle Walker
Club Tottenham
Right-back

Joleon Lescott
Club Man. City
Centre-back

Robin van Persie
Club Man. United
RATING 9/10

Lethal left foot – if he gets a shot on goal, he'll score!

Scott Parker
Club Tottenham
Midfielder

Papiss Cisse
Club Newcastle
Striker

MESSI FACT

Leo bagged 14 Champions League goals in 2011-12, making him the top scorer for the fourth season in a row!

MESSI V

LIONEL MESSI

CLUB: Barcelona
COUNTRY: Argentina
POSITION: Striker
AGE: 25
VALUE: £120 million
DID YOU KNOW? He scored an unbelievable 73 goals in all competitions in 2011-12!

MESSI	MEGA SKILLS	RONALDO
98	SHOOTING	97
97	DRIBBLING	96
97	FREE-KICKS	97
97	PENALTIES	96
94	HEADING	97
97	CROSSING	96
96	PASSING	96
97%	AVERAGE	96%

RONALDO FACT

C-Ron won his first La Liga title with Real Madrid in 2012 – to add to his three Prem titles with Man. United!

RONALDO

Who's the BEST?

WHAT DO YOU THINK?

Messi is the best!......... ✓

Ronaldo is the best!........ ✓

You've seen the evidence, now tell us who you think is the best!

CRISTIANO RONALDO

CLUB: Real Madrid
COUNTRY: Portugal
POSITION: Striker
AGE: 27
VALUE: £100 million
DID YOU KNOW? Ronaldo now wears Real's No.7 shirt after legend Raul left the club!

23

VAN PERSIE!
HIS AMAZING YEAR IN NUMBERS!

That's how many goals he scored for Arsenal and Holland last season!

44

22.5

That's how many millions United paid to sign him with another £1.5m in add-ons to come!

1

He won his first PFA Player Of The Year award in April!

30

He was the top scorer in the Premier League with a massive 30 goals!

23

He bagged his third MOTD Goal Of The Season with a cracker against Everton in December!

38

He has a reputation for getting injured but he played in all 38 Prem games for Arsenal last season!

v. PERSIE 20

24

2012 SUPERSTAR!

ETIHAD AIRWAYS

STAR FACTS

POSITION: Forward
VALUE: £40 million
DID YOU KNOW? Sergio
was Man. City Player
Of The Year for
2011-12!

AGUERO

MAN. CITY & ARGENTINA

AWESOME C

Write down the names of these players and fill in the

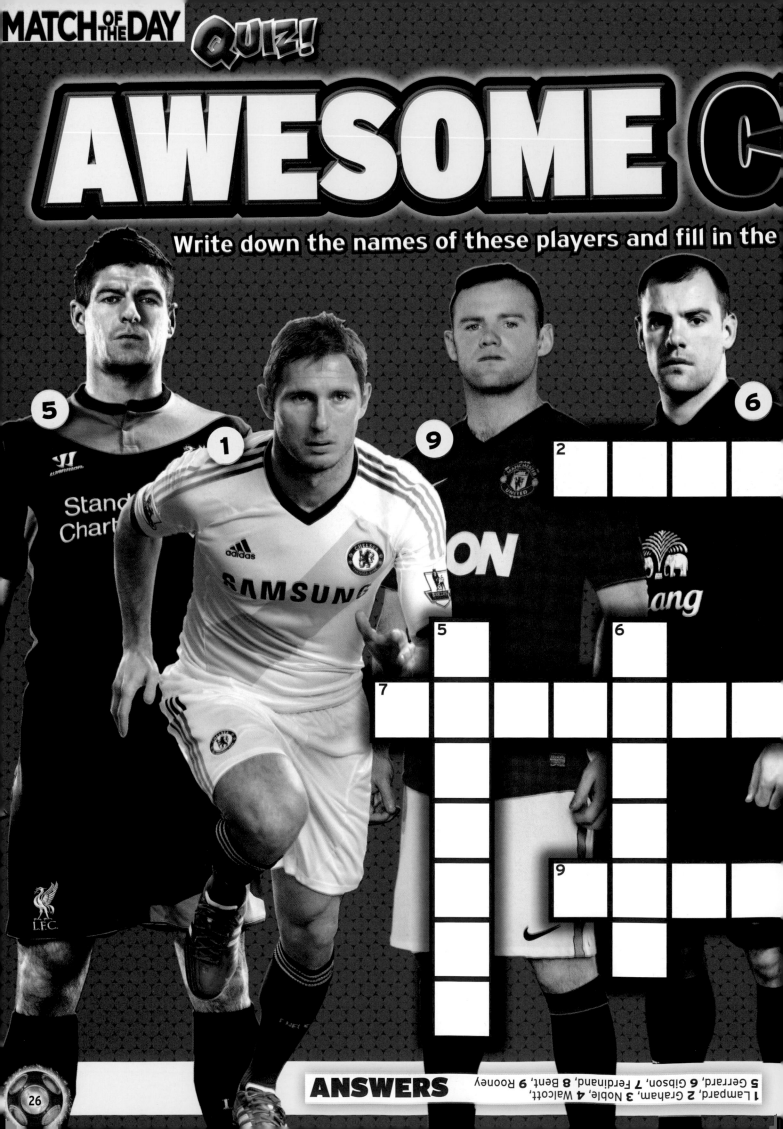

ANSWERS

1 Lampard, 2 Graham, 3 Noble, 4 Walcott, 5 Gerrard, 6 Gibson, 7 Ferdinand, 8 Bent, 9 Rooney

ROSSWORD!

grid. Pick up ten points for every name you get right!

1

Midfielder Andrea Pirlo looks like a grandad, but his magical midfield powers blasted Italy all the way to the Euro 2012 final!

2

England had a glimpse of the future when superkids Alex Oxlade-Chamberlain and Danny Welbeck showed off their wicked skills against France and Sweden!

15 REAS EURO 20

4

At last Ronaldo did the biz for Portugal, ripping Holland and Czech Republic to pieces! He had more shots on target than any other player!

5

Zlatan Ibrahimovic struck the MOTD Goal Of The Tournament with an incredible flying kick for Sweden against France!

ONS WHY 12 ROCKED!

3

Euro 2012 winners Spain finally proved they are the best national team ever. They blitzed this competition to win their third final in a row!

6

The Match of the Day cameras were at every single game, showing every goal, every tackle, every miss and every fan going bonkers. It was a complete TV footy fest!

7

Shock wins and shock stars, like Denmark beating Holland and Russia's Alan Dzagoev, helped make Euro 2012 one of the best finals ever!

Turn over for more EURO 2012!

15 REASONS WHY EURO 2012 ROCKED!

8

You couldn't take your eyes off City star Balotelli at the Euros. He was class and scored beauties against Rep. of Ireland and Germany!

9

England lost on penalties to Italy, but the penalty shoot-outs were packed with eye-popping excitement. Spain knocking out Portugal from the spot was mega!

12

Torres was awful for Chelsea for most of 2012, but he came to life for Spain in the summer and scored three goals to win the Golden Boot!

13

Euro 2012 threw up a few clashes between rival countries. Germany took on Holland, Portugal battled Spain and England tackled France!

10

Ukraine goal machine Andriy Shevchenko retired after Euro 2012, but he bowed out in style by scoring two awesome headers to help beat Sweden!

11

Germany lost to Italy in the semis, but they were still pretty special to watch this summer. We can't wait to see their big stars in the 2014 World Cup!

15

We loved watching the Euro 2012 mascots, Slavek and Slavko, jump around the pitch before and after games. They look like Jedward!

14

Spain's Andres Iniesta was crowned the player of the tournament. The clever midfielder had an amazing 90.5% passing accuracy!

Take the
MATCH OF TH

1 Which night is Match of the Day usually on TV?

MONDAY

SATURDAY

FRIDAY

2 Which year did Match of the Day first broadcast on television?

1954

1964

1984

3 Which of these is an expert pundit on Match of the Day?

ALAN HANSEN

STEVE WILSON

HARRY HILL

4 Where is Match of the Day filmed?

MANCHESTER

LONDON

BRISTOL

E DAY Test

How much do you know about the BIGGEST footy show on the planet?

5 When MOTD broadcasts from international tournaments, what's the programme called?

MATCH OF THE DAY MEGA

MATCH OF THE DAY NOW

MATCH OF THE DAY LIVE

6 Who is the host of Match of the Day 2?

DAN WALKER

COLIN MURRAY

ROBBIE SAVAGE

8 Which player lifts the Prem trophy at the end of the MOTD title sequence?

VINCENT KOMPANY

WAYNE ROONEY

JOHN TERRY

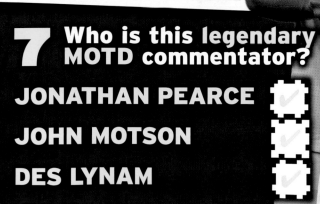

7 Who is this legendary MOTD commentator?

JONATHAN PEARCE

JOHN MOTSON

DES LYNAM

33

CRAZY CHEL

4 MARCH: Chelsea sack manager *Andre Villas-Boas* after some disappointing results, including defeats to Napoli and West Brom!

> Hey, I'm not rubbish really!

14 MARCH: After beating Birmingham and Stoke, new boss *Roberto Di Matteo* leads The Blues to a mega 4-1 win over Napoli in the Champions League!

15 APRIL: Di Matteo's Chelsea thump London rivals Tottenham 5-1 in the FA Cup semi-final. *Florent Malouda* scores the fifth!

2 MAY: Chelsea's hopes of finishing in the top four are dashed when Newcastle beat them 2-0. *Papiss Cisse* scores two stunners at The Bridge!

GOAL!

19 May: *Didier Drogba* is the hero again as he scores a late equaliser against Bayern Munich in the Champions League final...

> Have some of that!

...and *Drogba* scores the deciding penalty in the shoot-out as Chelsea finally win the Champions League!

GOAL!

SEA!

THE AMAZING STORY OF THEIR UNBELIEVABLE YEAR!

GOAL!

It's Nando time!

24 APRIL: Fernando Torres scores a superb late goal to help Chelsea knock out Barcelona in the Champions League to reach the final!

YESSSSS!

8 MAY: But just four days later, Liverpool smash them 4-1 in the Prem to end Chelsea's top-four dream!

GOAL!

Seeya!

5 MAY: Captain **John Terry** lifts the FA Cup after The Blues beat Liverpool in the final. Didier Drogba bags the crucial winning goal!

19 May: His goals help Chelsea to lift two shock trophies in a crazy season, and means they'll be in the Champions League!

19 June: Legendary striker **Drogba** says he's leaving Chelsea to play for Chinese club Shanghai Shenhua. The fans can't believe he's finally leaving!

SPOT THE DIFFERENCE!

Find all five differences to the picture at the bottom and pick up ten points for each one!

MY SCORE OUT OF 50

More Quiz Fun on p62!

MATCH OF THE DAY

2012 SUPERSTAR!

STAR FACTS

POSITION: Forward
VALUE: £120m
SUPER FACT: Messi has scored more goals for Barcelona than any other player!

MESSI

BARCELONA & ARGENTINA

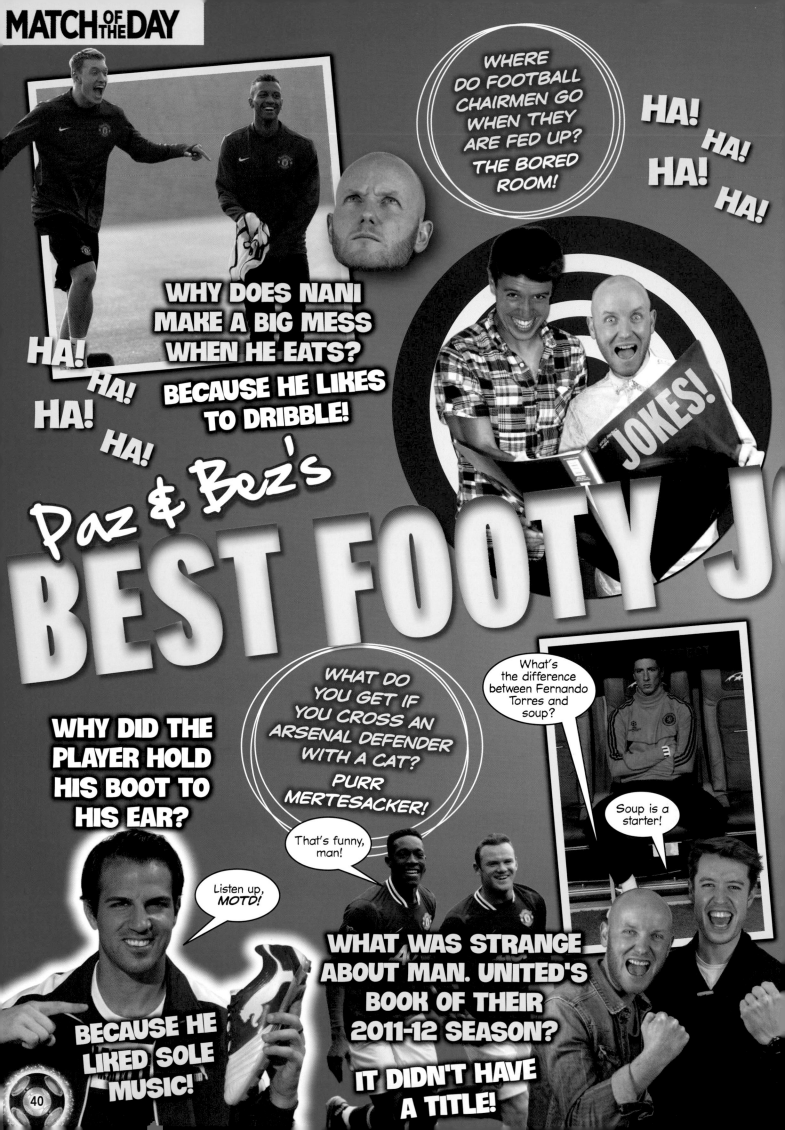

WHY IS CINDERELLA RUBBISH AT FOOTBALL? BECAUSE SHE RUNS AWAY FROM THE BALL!

WHAT DID THE BEE SAY AFTER HE BAGGED A GOAL?

HIVE HIT THE BACK OF THE NET!

WHERE DO SPIDERS PLAY FOOTBALL?

AT WEB-LEY STADIUM!

OKES OF 2012!

Do I look like I'm laughing, eh?

HA! HA! HA! HA!

HA! HA! HA! HA! HA!

WHY DOES ASHLEY COLE NOT LIKE TO SIGN AUTOGRAPHS?

BECAUSE HE CAN'T HANDLE A PEN!

HA! HA! HA! HA!

WHICH PLAYER MAKES HIS TEAM-MATES SMELL? JOEY FART-ON!

2012 SUPERSTAR!

STAR FACTS

POSITION: Forward
VALUE: £15m
DID YOU KNOW? Theo got 11 assists and eight goals in the Prem last season!

WALCOTT

ARSENAL & ENGLAND

2012 SUPERSTAR!

STAR FACTS

POSITION: Midfielder
VALUE: £8m
DID YOU KOW? Frank was Chelsea's top scorer last season, bagging 16 goals!

LAMPARD

CHELSEA & ENGLAND

That was *unbelievable!*

GOAL FACTS

WHO? Papiss Cisse, Newcastle
AGAINST? Chelsea
WHERE? Stamford Bridge
WHEN? 2 May 2012
WHAT HAPPENED? Cisse struck an amazing right-foot half-volley from the edge of the box that curled high over Petr Cech. Match of the Day picked it as the Goal Of The Season!

45

AGUERO FACT

Sergio was top scorer for Man. City last season with 23 goals in 34 Premier League matches!

AGUERO

SERGIO AGUERO

CLUB: Manchester City
COUNTRY: Argentina
POSITION: Striker
AGE: 24
VALUE: £35 million
DID YOU KNOW? Sergio is married to the daughter of Argentina footy legend Diego Maradona!

AGUERO	MEGA SKILLS	ROONEY
95	SHOOTING	96
96	DRIBBLING	94
95	FREE-KICKS	96
92	PENALTIES	95
91	HEADING	94
94	CROSSING	93
94	PASSING	95
94%	AVERAGE	95%

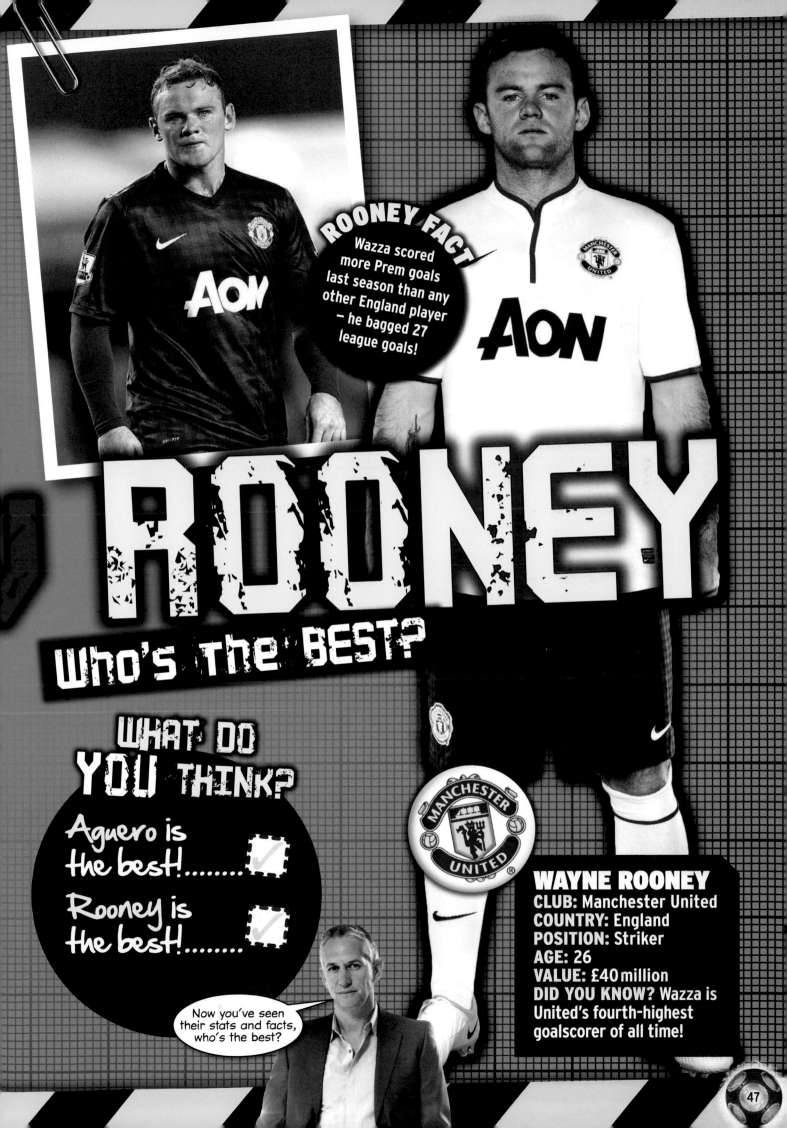

ROONEY FACT
Wazza scored more Prem goals last season than any other England player – he bagged 27 league goals!

ROONEY
Who's the BEST?

WHAT DO YOU THINK?

Aguero is the best!........ ✓

Rooney is the best!........ ✓

Now you've seen their stats and facts, who's the best?

WAYNE ROONEY
CLUB: Manchester United
COUNTRY: England
POSITION: Striker
AGE: 26
VALUE: £40 million
DID YOU KNOW? Wazza is United's fourth-highest goalscorer of all time!

47

MANCHESTER CITY

Premier League champions 2011-12

2012 SUPERSTAR!

STAR FACTS

POSITION: Midfielder
VALUE: £35m
DID YOU KNOW? Cesc scored two goals at Euro 2012 for Spain!

FABREGAS

BARCELONA & SPAIN

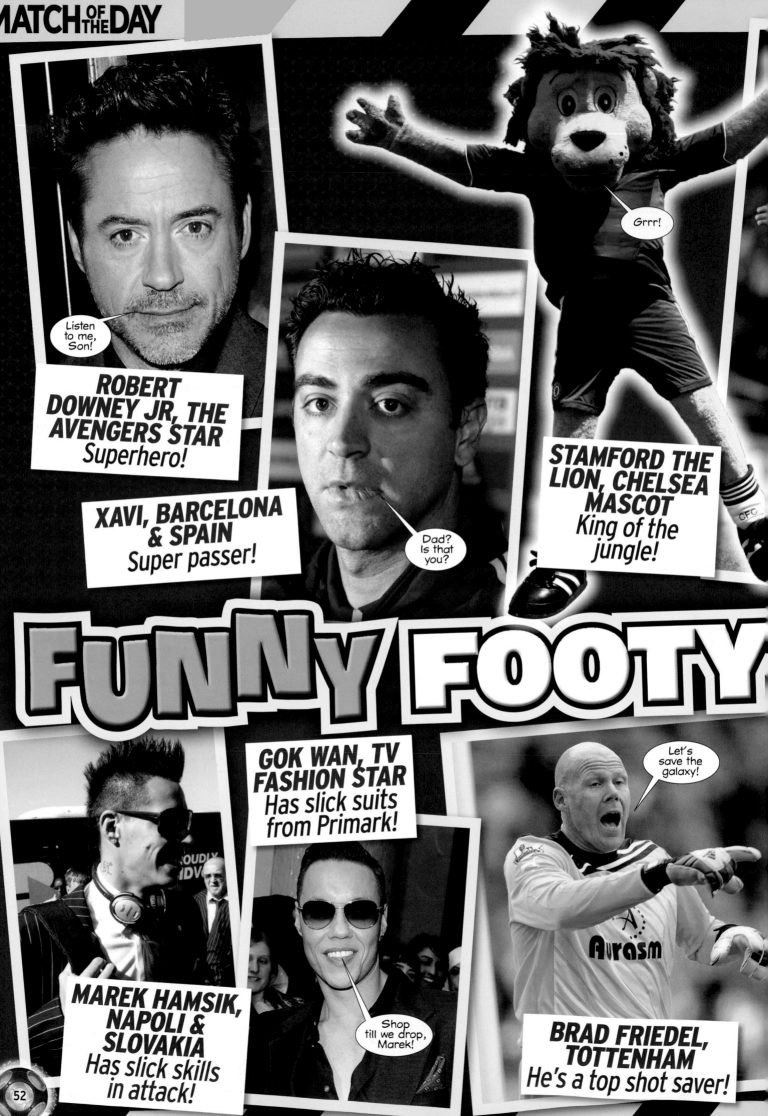

Grrr!

Listen to me, Son!

ROBERT DOWNEY JR, THE AVENGERS STAR
Superhero!

XAVI, BARCELONA & SPAIN
Super passer!

Dad? Is that you?

STAMFORD THE LION, CHELSEA MASCOT
King of the jungle!

FUNNY FOOTY

GOK WAN, TV FASHION STAR
Has slick suits from Primark!

Let's save the galaxy!

Shop till we drop, Marek!

MAREK HAMSIK, NAPOLI & SLOVAKIA
Has slick skills in attack!

BRAD FRIEDEL, TOTTENHAM
He's a top shot saver!

WIN THE MOT

61 **62** **63** **64**

65 The whole team rows on the pitch! Go back nine spaces

60 **59**

58 That's the Goal of the Season! Move forward five spaces

57 **56**

41 **42** **43** **44** **45**

40

39 Rumours that you'll spend millions on a new player! Move forward three spaces

38 Floodlight failure at your ground! Go back two spaces

37 **36**

21 **22** **23** **24**

25 Your game is postponed due to bad weather! Go back three spaces

20 You sign a new player! Move forward four spaces

17 **19** **18** **17**

16 Alan Hansen slams your team on MOTD! Go back ten spaces

KICK-OFF!
1 The ref blows the whistle – the action begins!

2

3 You win your first game of the season! Move forward seven spaces

4 **5**

D CUP!

Grab a mate and play the game to see who wins!

HOW TO PLAY!
- You need: a counter (this could be a coin) and a dice!
- Roll the dice to see how many squares you move forward!
- The first person to reach the last square lifts the cup!

70

WELL DONE! YOU'VE WON THE CUP!

66

67

68
Missed penalty! Go back nine spaces

69

55
A 2-0 loss to the bottom team! Go back to square 43

54

53
You score a last-minute winner against the champions! Move forward seven spaces

52

51
You lose five games in a row! Go back 20 spaces

46

47
You score the MOTD Goal of the Month! Move forward five spaces

48

49

50

35
A 3-0 win over your local rivals! Take another turn

34
Your best youngster is called up for his country! Move forward three spaces

33

32

31

26

27

28
Your manager gets a new long-term contract! Take another turn

29

30
Your star striker wins the MOTD Player Of The Month! Move forward three spaces

MATCH DAY
PAPISS CISSE!

15

14

13
Your captain is sent off! Miss a turn

12

11
You get your biggest crowd of the season! Take another turn

6

7
Your keeper makes a big mistake! Go back to the start

8

9

10

1

KAGAWA
26

New Man. United superstar **Shinji Kagawa** was too scared to wear the club's famous **No.7** shirt!

2

A few weeks after Chelsea signed **Eden Hazard** this year, they snapped us his younger brother **Thorgan** too!

3

Fabregas spoke to the ball before he struck Spain's winning penalty against Portugal at **Euro 2012**!

DID YOU

50 FAB FOOTY FACT

7

New Arsenal star **Lukas Podolski** played his **100th** game for Germany at Euro 2012, and scored his 44th international goal!

8

Ashley Cole won a record **seventh FA Cup final**!

9

Stoke's **Ryan Shotton** had a **secret towel** stitched under his shirt so he could wipe the ball and throw it further!

10

New QPR boss **Mark Hughes** tried to buy **Tevez** from Man. City this year!

5

Mexico scored after just **28 seconds** as they won gold against Brazil at the London 2012 Olympics!

6

4

Newcastle boss **Alan Pardew** gave star striker **Papiss Cisse** a special goat curry, and in the next game he scored twice against Liverpool!

England rose to **third** in FIFA's world rankings this year – their highest ever position!

KNOW?

S & SECRETS OF 2012!

You can check out the ace Gareth Bale cartoon on p72, but the Spurs hero told us that he loves his Super Bale character!

14

13

11

Aston Villa goal machine **Darren Bent** bagged his **100th** Premier League goal!

Man. City striker **David Guidetti** scored 20 goals on loan for Feyenoord last season, despite hardly anyone knowing who he was!

In 2012, **Man. United** didn't win a trophy. The last time that happened was back in **2005**!

12

TURN OVER FOR MORE FACTS!

DID YOU KNOW?

50 FAB FOOTY FACTS & SECRETS OF 2012!

16
Portsmouth played with ten outfield players aged **18 years and under** in the first game of the season against Plymouth!

17
BBC pundit **Robbie Savage** offered to come out of retirement to play for **Rangers** in the Scottish fourth tier!

15
Aston Villa keeper **Shay Given** retired from Republic of Ireland this summer after playing a record **125 games!**

22
Birmingham keeper **Jack Butland** became the youngest keeper to play for England, aged just 19!

21
Newcastle trio **Ryan Taylor, Hatem Ben Arfa** and **Papiss Cisse** all won MOTD Goal Of The Month awards!

26
Torres finally scored a hat-trick for Chelsea in 2012 – it was his **63rd** game for the club!

27
Southampton smashed their transfer record twice in 2012, paying £7 million for **Rodriguez** and then £11.8 million for **Ramirez!**

28

Spurs defender **Kyle Walker** shocked Sergio Aguero and Gareth Bale to win the **PFA Young Player of the Year!**

18

Lionel Messi scored **five goals** in just one Champions League game against Bayer Leverkusen!

20

City won **20** home Premier League games in a row between March 2011 and March 2012!

19

Aston Villa drew **17 Prem** games last season, a joint record with Newcastle!

23

Amazingly the Olympics was the **first** international tournament that **Ryan Giggs** had ever played in!

24

Everton sold **Steven Pienaar** to Spurs for £3 million in 2011, but they bought him back for **£4.5 million** in 2012. Not great business!

25

When **Zlatan Ibrahimovic** moved to PSG, his total transfer fees in his career hit nearly **£130 million**!

29

Van Persie was the first Arsenal player to transfer to Man. United in **25 years**!

30

West Ham, Southampton, Fulham and **Blackburn** all made bids to buy **red-hot** Huddersfield striker **Jordan Rhodes**!

31

Cardiff's home kit changed from their famous blue to red – their nickname is **The Bluebirds**!

32

Sunderland smashed their transfer record by signing **Steven Fletcher** from Wolves for **£15 million**!

TURN OVER FOR MORE FACTS!

59

DID YOU KNOW?

50 FAB FOOTY FACTS & SECRETS OF 2012!

33

Djibril Cisse made a big impact at QPR – in his first eight games he scored six goals and got two red cards!

34

AC Milan pals Robinho and Kevin Prince-Boateng spent ages working on this dance-routine goal celebration!

35

Norwich keeper John Ruddy missed out on his first England cap against Belgium because he got married on the same day!

39

Striker Nicolas Anelka joined Chinese side Shanghai Shenua in January, then in April he was made player-manager in a shock move!

40

Amazingly, at Euro 2012 Wayne Rooney scored his first tournament goal for England in eight years!

41

Everton defender Tony Hibbert finally scored his first goal for the club in a pre-season friendly – it was his 308th game for The Toffees!

45

Gareth Bale spoke about how he doesn't like Charlie Adam very much after the pair clashed in a friendly!

46

Real Madrid won Spain's La Liga with a record 100 points!

47

Hugo Rodallega joined Fulham, but he left Wigan with the record of being their all-time leading scorer in the Prem – with just 24 goals!

36

Chelsea won £47.3m in prize money for winning the Champions League final in 2012!

37

Olympic champion **Usain Bolt** said he reckons he's got the skills to play for **Man. United!**

38

Golf fan **Carlos Tevez** was the caddy for Argentina's **Andres Romero** at The Open this summer!

42

England keeper **Joe Hart** pulled freaky faces at the Italy players before they took penalties in the shoot-out at **Euro 2012** – but England still lost!

43

Chelsea's **Ashley Cole** gave his **Community Shield** runners-up medal to a surprised Man. City fan in the crowd at the game!

44

Nikija Jelavic was the top scorer for both **Everton** and **Rangers** in 2011-12!

48

Last season, **Sergio Aguero** wore secret blacked-out boots before he signed a massive deal with **Puma!**

49

Tottenham and **Real Madrid** announced they had signed a deal to work together and share football knowledge and ideas!

50

David Beckham signed a new two-year contract with LA Galaxy after turning down a move to **PSG** in France!

NAME THE YEAR!

Write down which year these happened – it's five points for each correct one!

1

THE YEAR WAS ANSWER

2

MANCHESTER UNITED 8   5:52
ARSENAL   2   0:00

THE YEAR WAS ANSWER

2012

2010

CHOOSE FROM YEARS...

2011

2008

3

THE YEAR WAS ANSWER

4

THE YEAR WAS ANSWER

ANSWERS: 1 2008, 2 2011, 3 2012, 4 2010.

MY SCORE OUT OF 20

More Quiz Fun on p80!

2012 SUPERSTAR!

STAR FACTS

POSITION: Striker
VALUE: £35m
DID YOU KNOW? Neymar scored three goals at the 2012 Olympics!

NEYMAR

SANTOS & BRAZIL

LINEKER

"MY FOOTY FACTS & STATS!"

3 Lineker finished as the highest scorer in England's top league three times – in 1985, 1986 and 1990!

Check out my hair!

18 That's how old Gary was when he made his debut for Leicester, the team he'd supported since he was a little kid!

1 Despite all the goals and records he broke, Lineker won only one major trophy in England – when Spurs lifted the FA Cup in 1991!

Er, who shrunk the FA Cup, guys?

6 At the World Cup in 1986, Gary won the Golden Shoe as the competition's top scorer with six goals. Even Messi has never won this award!

LOOK, IT'S GARY!

£2.8million

Barcelona paid Everton a huge £2.8million to sign Gary in 1986. Today, that's the same as about £30million!

GOAL!

28

Lineker scored the second quickest hat-trick ever at a World Cup finals when he bagged three against Poland in 1986 in just 28 minutes!

0

Even though he played nearly 600 games in his career, he was never even booked or sent off. The refs really loved Gary!

5

Gary played for five clubs in his career. He started with Leicester before going to Everton, Barcelona, Tottenham and Grampus Eight!

4

He twice scored four goals in a single game for England. Amazingly, one of those games was against Spain in Madrid!

48

That's how many goals MOTD presenter Lineker scored for England. He's the second highest scorer ever!

Read more about me and the *MOTD* boys on p32!

2012 SUPERSTAR!

STAR FACTS

POSITION: Striker
VALUE: £20m
DID YOU KNOW? Robin won the Prem Golden Boot in 2011-12 with 30 goals!

VAN PERSIE

MAN. UNITED & HOLLAND

2012 SUPERSTAR!

STAR FACTS

POSITION: Midfielder
VALUE: £10m
DID YOU KNOW? Steven got three assists for England at Euro 2012!

GERRARD

LIVERPOOL & ENGLAND

MATCH OF THE DAY
KICKABOUT

WHAT IS IT?

Match of the Day Kickabout is the hottest weekly footy TV show for young fans!

WHAT'S ON IT?

Top stars, celebrity guests, funny interviews, skills tips, goal action and more!

WHO PRESENTS IT?

A crazy bloke called Ore – he's nuts about footy and loves meeting up with the game's biggest heroes. MOTD mag reporters Paz & Bez appear on the show all the time too!

CHECK OUT WHAT'S ON THE SHOW...

This is the part of the show when the special guest is tested on their expert knowledge. They watch some action and then have to answer Ore's brain-busting questions!

Ore's HALF TIME CHALLENGE

The Top 5 includes anything and everything to do with footy – from left-backs to legends, keepers to blunders. Ore always has loads of fun picking out his favourites every week!

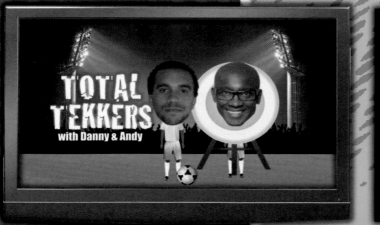

TOTAL TEKKERS
with Danny & Andy

MOTD Kickabout teaches you the coolest skills, tips and tricks! Total Tekkers shows you how to do lots of ace stuff, with the help of experts Danny Edwards and Andy Ansah!

WALL

Catch me every Saturday, Kickabout fans!

MEET ORE!

THE TOP 5

In the Kickabout Wall Of Fame, Ore and his guest pick out a legend to add to the star-studded wall. But watch out for some strange entries too, like Emile Heskey and Tony Hibbert!

BEHIND THE SCENES WITH PAZ & BEZ

READING THE RIOT ACT!
Paz & Bez pop up on the Kickabout TV screen all the time – here they are barking instructions at the Reading players!

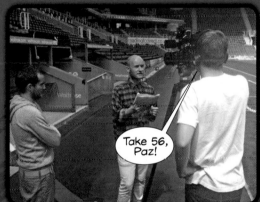

No, shoot that way!

CAMERA CRAZY!
Here's Paz practising his lines to the camera – try not to make any mistakes, mate!

Take 56, Paz!

BEZ WALKS THE TALK!
Bez has to walk and talk at the same time as he films at West Ham's Upton Park. It's a tough job, hey?

Left, right, left, right...

NEW SAINTS STAR?
Sometimes, the lads forget that they aren't real footy players. Here's Bez pretending that he's just signed for Southampton!

Who wants an autograph?

STAR FACTS

POSITION: Striker
VALUE: £18m
DID YOU KNOW? Danny got England's winner against Sweden at Euro 2012!

WELBECK

MAN. UNITED & ENGLAND

Ronny! Where are ya?

NANI TO REAL MADRID
After six years in England, surely the Man. United winger would jump at the chance to hook up with old pal Ronaldo in La Liga!

IT WILL HAPPEN! ✓   IT WON'T HAPPEN! ✗

LAMPARD TO LA GALAXY
Super Franky Lampard is a legend for The Blues, but maybe it's now time for him to get some time in the sun and show off his skills in California!

IT WILL HAPPEN! ✓   IT WON'T HAPPEN! ✗

BIG MOVES

Will these transfers actually happen next year?

WALCOTT TO CHELSEA
The rumour is that Walcott came really close to leaving Arsenal in the summer – will he be Chelsea's big signing come January?

IT WILL HAPPEN! ✓   IT WON'T HAPPEN! ✗

RUBBISH A[V]

RUBBISH TRANSFER

I've not even been to the Chelsea canteen!

KEVIN DE BRUYNE

De Bruyne joined Chelsea for £7 million in January, but was instantly loaned back to Racing Genk before he was loaned again to Werder Bremen in August. He hasn't played a proper game for Chelsea!

This shirt makes me sick!

RUBBISH CELEBRATION

This game's rubbish, anyway!

MAN. CITY FANS

City fans still do the Poznan celebration after scoring — they turn around and jump up and down. How can you watch the game doing that, you muppets?

RUBBISH 17 MINUTES

WOJCIECH SZCZESNY

The Arsenal keeper mucked up to let Greece equalise against Poland at Euro 2012 — then he was sent off 17 minutes later and missed the rest of the competition!

78

RUBBISH KIT

BARCELONA

Wow! You need sunglasses on to look at this shocking strip! It looks like Messi has left his kit in the sun too long, and then threw up on it. Ugh!

Can we play you every week, Scholesy?

Shut up and get your hair cut!

RUBBISH TEAM TO PLAY

MAN. UNITED v EVERTON

United hated playing Everton in 2012! They suffered a shock 1-0 loss in the first game of this season and a 4-4 draw in April that helped hand the title to City!

Stop laughing at me, MOTD!

WARDS 2012!

My brother's called Mouldy Solbakken!

RUBBISH HAIR

WAYNE ROONEY

Wazza has been trying to grow his mop top all year after having a hair transplant. Sorry dude, but it still looks ridiculous!

RUBBISH NAME

STALE SOLBAKKEN

The new Wolves manager sounds like a loaf of bread that will give you a dodgy tummy!

RUBBISH TATTOO

DANIELE DE ROSSI

The Italy midfielder showed off this crazy tat at Euro 2012. Is that him crunching in to a tough tackle? It's well rubbish, mate!

QUIZ!

FOOTY HE

Can you match the correct heads to the correct

ANSWERS

STAR FACTS

POSITION: Midfielder
VALUE: £33m
DID YOU KNOW? Luka
joined Real from Spurs
for £33m in August
2012!

MODRIC

REAL MADRID & CROATIA

2012 SUPERSTAR!

STAR FACTS

POSITION: Midfielder
VALUE: £10m
DID YOU KNOW? Andrea won Serie A in 2012 – his first season at Juve!

PIRLO

JUVENTUS & ITALY

 **2012 SUPERSTAR!**

STAR FACTS

POSITION: Striker
VALUE: £18.1m
DID YOU KNOW? Zlatan and Thiago Silva left Milan for PSG for £51 million!

IBRAHIMOVIC

 **PSG & SWEDEN**

FIND THE M

MOTD stars Lineker, Hansen, Shearer, Lawro and Murray are hidin

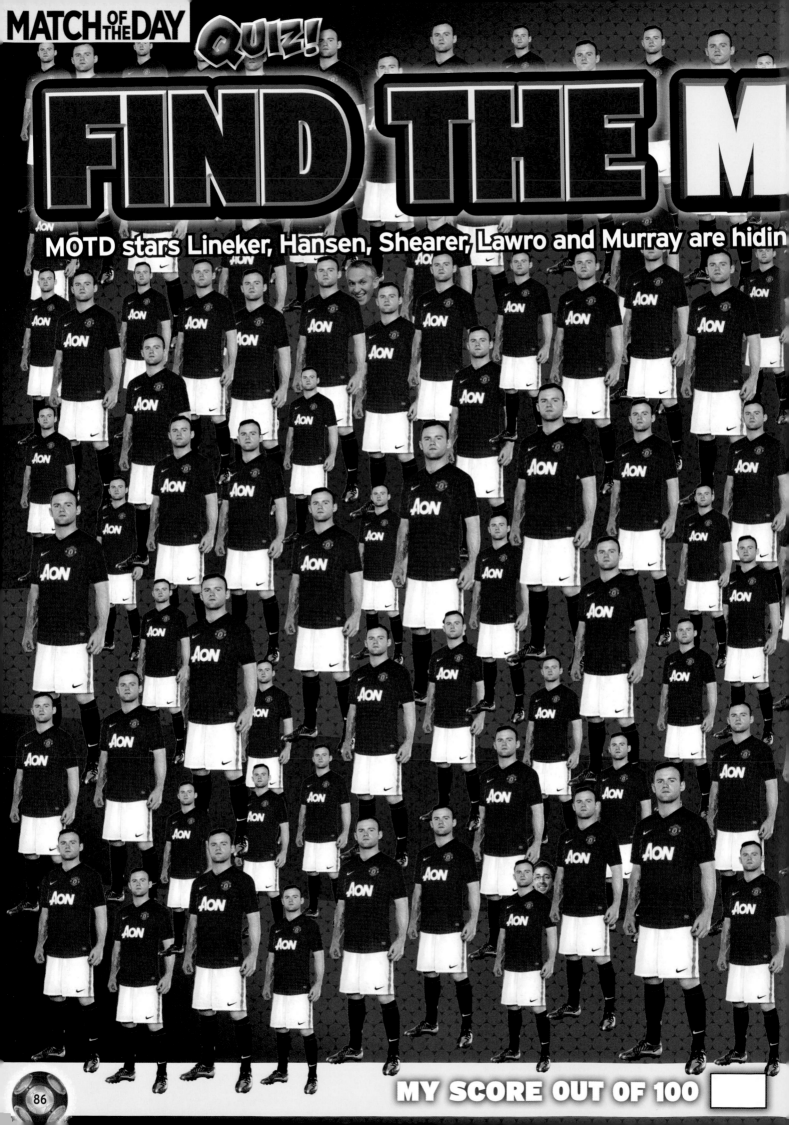

MY SCORE OUT OF 100

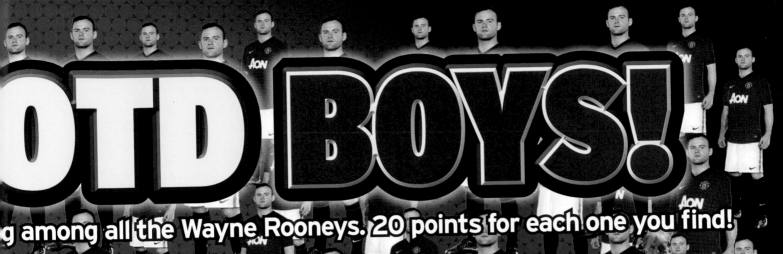

OTD BOYS!

...g among all the Wayne Rooneys. 20 points for each one you find!

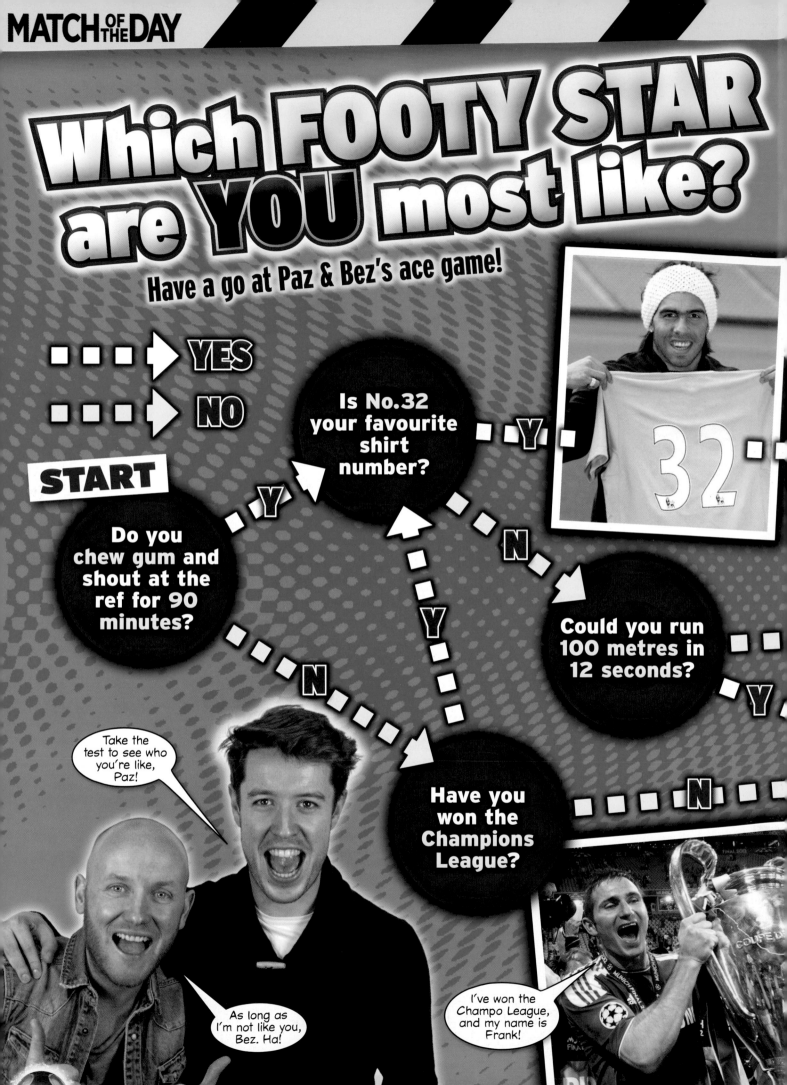

Which FOOTY STAR are YOU most like?

Have a go at Paz & Bez's ace game!

- ■ ■ ■ ▶ **YES**
- ■ ■ ■ ▶ **NO**

START

Do you chew gum and shout at the ref for 90 minutes?

Is No.32 your favourite shirt number?

Could you run 100 metres in 12 seconds?

Have you won the Champions League?

Take the test to see who you're like, Paz!

As long as I'm not like you, Bez. Ha!

I've won the Champo League, and my name is Frank!

88

Have you ever flown to Argentina to play golf during the season?

Y →

Do Man. United fans think you are a footy god?

N → You are... CARLOS TEVEZ! You've had clashes with managers and fans, but you're world class and helped Man. City win the league. Just put your golf clubs down and score more goals!

N ↓ (from Have you ever flown to Argentina)

Y ↓

N → Has the Queen made you a Sir?

N (from Do Man. United fans think you are a footy god)

Has the Queen made you a Sir?

Y → You are... SIR ALEX FERGUSON! You can be a bit of a grump, but all the Man. United players and fans love you – you've won about a million trophies for the club!

Do you take ages to do your hair?

N →

Y ↓

Is your middle name Frank?

N ↑

Y → You are... GARETH BALE! You're the Prem's most exciting superstar – every club on the planet wants to buy you. Just don't mess your hair up, okay!

MATCH OF THE DAY

YOUR QUIZ SCORE!

Add up all your scores from the quizzes
– and see what your total score is!

0-150 POINTS
TRANSFER LISTED!
The club don't want you any more – you're out of here!

151-250 POINTS
NEW STAR!
Not too bad – keep reading MOTD and you'll be a quiz star!

251-400 POINTS
PREM FAVE!
Top effort – you're showing Champions League form, dude!

401-540 POINTS
WORLD HERO!
Awesome score, bruv! You showed the world your slick quiz skills!

MY TOTAL SCORE IS .... /540

2012 SUPERSTAR!

STAR FACTS

POSITION: Striker
VALUE: £30m
DID YOU KNOW? Mario won his fourth league title in 2012!

BALOTELLI

MAN. CITY & ITALY

MY 2013 F PREDICT

Tell us who you think the footy heroes will be

THE PREMIER LEAGUE TOP SCORER WILL BE...

Wayne Rooney ✓

Sergio Aguero ✓

Papiss Cisse ✓

Other

THE CHAMPIONS LEAGUE WINNERS WILL BE...

Barcelona ✓

Real Madrid ✓

Man. United ✓

Juventus ✓

Other

THE PREMIER LEAGUE CHAMPIONS WILL BE...

Man. City ✓

Man. United ✓

Chelsea ✓

Arsenal ✓

Other